SALLY CRAVENS

How Much is My Company?

A Beginner's Guide to Valuation Methods

First edition

This book was professionally typeset on Reedsy.
Find out more at reedsy.com

Contents

1

Introduction

How much is my company worth? If you are a business owner, you must have thought about this at least once or twice. It is the same for a stock investor. How much is my stock really worth? Is it time to buy or sell?

Many professionals can provide you with the "answers" to these questions. The financial consultants and the 7-figure salary stock analysts do this daily. However, if you don't understand the methods and the tools that they use, how do you determine whether the answers they provide you are the "right answers?"

In this book, I will explain the basics behind the valuation methods that the professionals use to give you their recommendations. Not the long and lengthy text book-like explanations, but the simple logic behind each method, so that you can use them to value your business or stock. Or, at least understand what the professionals are talking about when they are throwing out the big words at you.

I hope that after reading this book, you can start forming your own opinion about what your business is worth, or what the price of your stock should be.

2

Why Do I Need to Know Valuation Methods?

Whether you are a small business owner or an investor in the stock market, you don't want to make uninformed decisions, whether the results are good or bad. Many times, you will get better results by listening to those who know what they are talking about. However, since there are so many opinions out there by those who "know what they are talking about," how do you know which one to listen to? In addition, these opinions may be all different, although they are all formed using the same information available. Then who do you listen to?

At the end of the day, it is always your money, not theirs. I am not recommending that you don't listen to professional opinions or recommendations. I am proposing that you understand what the recommendations are and how they were formed. This will help you make your decisions. The results of your decisions may not be perfect, but the decisions will be informed decisions that you can build on, rather than relying on luck.

Private Business Owners

If you have your own business, you may be faced with situations in which you need to understand the value of your company. Someone may offer to buy your company. Someone may offer to sell you his or her business. If you wish to exit from your business or expand, you may consider the offers. But then, for how much?

You may hire a financial or business consultant to value your company, but is the price right? Many of the consultants work on a success fee basis, in which they will get the big payout if the deal goes through. Therefore, their interests may not align with your interests. You want to get the best price for the business that you have built, but the consultants want to recommend a price that the buyer likes, which may be lower than what your business is worth. Or if you are buying a business, the consultants may lead you to believe that the seller's price is a bargain.

Sometimes, your business is too small to even hire a professional consultant. Then how do you determine whether the offer is right?

You may also be stuck on a price that may not be correct. "I need at least 1 million dollars to retire, so I am going to wait until somebody offers me at least 1 million dollars for my business." Instead, it might be better to sell your business at $700,000 and then reinvest to make the 1 million dollars that you need.

Whether you are buying or selling, or just want to get a grasp of the price for future reference, you want to know how the valuation is done so that you can form your own opinion. Even if you get professional assistance, you can have more meaningful discussions with your consultants and make better informed decisions, if you understand the valuation methods.

Investors in the Stock Market

The valuation methods that are used to determine a target price of a traded stock is the same as the valuation methods that you use in valuing a private company. You just don't own the entire 100% of the company. You own only a part of the company, whether 1% or 0.0001%.

If you are an investor in the stock market, you make decisions all the time. To buy or to sell. Or to hold. Even if you hold your position and don't take any actions, it still is a decision you made. So how do you make these decisions? If you take away your investment horizon and your portfolio strategy, you make your decision based on the "value," or the target price of the stock relative to the current market price.

If you think that publicly traded Company A is worth $100 a share, and the current market price is only $70 a share, you buy before the market reflects the value of the company at $100 per share. When it does, you can make $30 per share. If the current market price is $130, then you want to sell before the price drops to $100 per share. These are the recommendations that you would make if you value the company at $100 a share.

Suppose you have 10 shares of Company A, and the current market price is $70 a share. Then you hear in the news that a renowned stock analyst is recommending that you buy this stock. You say to yourself, "Great. I am going to buy 10 more shares." So you open your laptop and log in to your trading site. Then you see that the price is already at $80. Do you still buy the 10 shares? Or do you sell the 10 shares that you already own? Or do you hold? These are the questions that you won't be able to answer if you don't have a grasp of the valuation method that the analyst used. If you value the share at $100 given the available current information, and you agree with the valuation method that the analyst has used, then you would still buy the 10 shares.

3

Equity Value

When you value your business or a stock, you are looking at the equity value of the company. The equity value is what belongs to you, or the shareholders.

Equity Value = Enterprise Value - Debt

The "enterprise value" is the total value of your company. If you don't have any debt, then your enterprise value is your equity value.

Suppose you are selling the restaurant that you own. The restaurant is valued at $700,000, your Enterprise Value. The company has a $200,000 loan from the bank, the only debt the company has. Then your company's equity value is $500,000, and you would sell the company at $500,000 with the debt. Or you can sell the business assets for $700,000, then pay back the loan yourself. You will still end up with $500,000 in equity value.

The valuation models that I will go over in the next 3 chapters will mostly focus on determining the Enterprise Value of the business. Depending on the assumptions and the methods used, the Enterprise Value will vary. However, focus on the methods used and the logic behind each method. This will help you determine which method is more applicable to your situation and how to apply the method to your company or stock.

4

Discounted Cash Flow Method

T he Discounted Cash Flow Method, or "DCF," is the
most commonly used valuation method. It is unique
to the business that you are valuing and can be applied
to just about any business, whether it is a farm or a restaurant
or a biotech company. All you need is the projected future
cash flow and the discount rate. I will explain both of them
below, but once you have the two, you can get the value of your
company.

This method is also the most dangerous method to use due to
the many assumptions that the method requires. Sometimes
you can fall into the trap of predetermining the price and
playing with the assumptions in the model to end up with that
set price.

So, if you are building the model for yourself, be honest. If you
are reviewing someone else's model, watch out for the tricky
assumptions. You can plug in your own assumptions in that
model to see what the value comes out to.

Present Value

The discounted cash flow is the way to determine the Present Value of the cash flow the business will generate in the future. What is a present value? It is the value of a cash flow from today's perspective, accounting for the time value of money.

$100 today is different from $100 one year from now. Suppose you invested $100 one year ago in a stock called Company A. Today, the price is still $100. You did not lose money. However, had you borrowed that $100 from a bank at 6% interest rate, you actually lost $6 in paying the interest. Or, if you had put that $100 in your savings account, you could have made $3 from the interest earned. Therefore, $100 one year ago is not the same as $100 today.

The same goes for the future cash flow. If you invest in a product that gives you $100 every year, the $100 today is different from the $100 you will get 1 year from now. That $100 is different from the $100 you will get 2 years from now.

The formula for discounting cash flow is as follows:

Discounted cash flow = CFt / (1+r)^t
   CFt - Cash flow (t) years from now
   r - discount rate
   t - time from the beginning of the period

Suppose you are expected to receive $100 one year from now. And the discount rate used in discounting the cash flow is 10%. Then the formula applied is

$$100 / (1+ 0.10)\ ^\wedge\ 1$$

The discounted cash flow, or the present value of the $100 one year from now is $90.1.

Projection

The cash flow from the business that you have or the company you invest in will not be as simple as the one from the above example. Not only would the company generate cash flows in multiple years, but they will also likely be all different.

So to value a company, you need to project the future cash flow of all future years. Once you determine them, you can apply the above formula for each future years' cash flow to get their present value, and add them up to get the value of your company.

To do this, you need to project out all cash items of your business, including the revenue, all components of the costs, and the investments to be made. This is usually done in an Excel spreadsheet. If you are not good with Excel, you may need to get help from a consultant, but know that this the concept applied when they are talking about the discounted cash flow method to determine your company's value

Free Cash Flow

Once you have the projected cash flow, you do not use that

as the future cash flow to determine the present value of your company. What you use is a Free Cash Flow, or "FCF". FCF is just adjusting the operating cash flow with the investments made.

Suppose you own a restaurant, and you made $100,000 last year. If you do not make any investments and there are no changes in the market, you can expect to make $100,000 next year. However, if you make a $500,000 investment in expanding your restaurant with additional seats, you can expect a higher cash flow in the future years. Suppose you increase your seating space by 50%, you can expect to make $150,000, assuming the same cost structure with no scalability.

The new cash flow projection will be a lot higher and the value of your company, or the present value of your company's cash flow, will be a lot higher as well. Therefore, to get to your cash flow to value your company, you need to adjust the future cash flow by subtracting the investments made each year. This will give you the Free Cash Flow of your company.

Discount Rate

Now that you have your future Free Cash Flow, you need to apply the discount rate to "discount" the future Cash flow into their present value.

The discount rate can vary depending on the business. The

discount rate should reflect the inherent riskiness of the business. In the above example of borrowing $100 at 6% interest rate to invest in Company A stock, you may think to apply the 6% as your discount rate. However, that 6% interest rate reflects your credit risk that the bank sees, not the inherent risk of Company A. If you are trying to determine the value of Company A, you need to determine the discount rate for Company A, not yours.

The discount rate used should be the Weighted Average Cost of Capital, or a "WACC" of the company. The formula for the WACC is as follows:

WACC = Ke X E/(E+D) + Kd X D/(E+D) * (1-t)
  Ke - Cost of Equity
  Kd - Cost of Debt
  E - Equity Amount
  D - Debt Amount
  t - Tax Rate

The cost of capital is basically how much you need to pay to get the funding done for the business. This will reflect the inherent risk of the company.

Suppose that Company A is using 50% Debt and 50% Equity to fund the company. If the company has one simple loan from a bank, and it is paying a 9% interest rate, the Kd, or the cost of debt, is 9%.

Cost of equity is a bit more tricky. There are models you can use, such as CAPM using the Beta of the industry. However, simply put, the cost of equity, Ke, is how much an equity investor should get paid for their investment risk. This is always going to be higher than the cost of debt, Kd. If a company is liquidated, the debt holders get paid first, then the leftover will be given to the equity holders. Therefore, the equity risk is always higher.

The tax effect is applied to the cost of debt, due to corporate tax savings that the company gets from making the interest payments on the debt.

Suppose the Ke for Company A is 15% and the tax rate is 21%. Then the WACC is calculated to be:

$$15\% \times (50/100) + 9\% \times (50/100)*(1 - 0.21) = 11.055\%$$

This is the discount rate you would use for Company A.

Debt to Equity Ratio

One area that you need to be careful with is the Debt and Equity ratio. The ratio to be used is not the actual ratio but the ideal ratio that reflects the risk of the business.

For example, suppose there are two exactly the same companies, but financed differently. One with 30% debt, and one with 50% debt. If you apply these current debt levels, then the two companies with the exact same future operating cash flow will have two different WACCs to generate two different valuations. Also, you have to separate your credit from the company's risk, especially if you have your own business. If you were able to 70% debt finance this company using your credit, and you use this as the debt ratio, the WACC will not reflect the true risk of the company, which may be only 50%.

Then how do you determine the debt to equity ratio that reflects the business? The basic tool used is the coverage ratio. A coverage ratio is how many times your business's operating cash flow can "cover" your interest payment. The banks always want to make sure that you make their interest payments. Every year, your operating cash flow will vary. It can go up, or it can go down. So the banks, when they make the decision on how much to lend you, will take a look at your operating cash flow and how many times it can cover the interest payment, or the coverage ratio. If the cash flow is very consistent every year, the bank may require a lower coverage ratio, such as 2X. However, if it fluctuates greatly, then the ratio may be in the 5X range or higher.

Based on this ratio, you can determine the total debt you can carry on your balance sheet. The coverage ratio is not something that you determine. It is determined by the lending institutions based on your company's credit risk and their credit appetite.

Suppose Company A is generating $100,000 operating cash flow per year, and the banks apply a 3X coverage ratio in the industry you are in. Then the banks will not lend you a loan that will have more than ⅓ of the operating cash flow in interest payments, or $33,333. So if you can pay a maximum of $33,333 per year in interest payment and your interest rate is 9%, the total loan that you can get from a bank is $33,333 divided by 9%, or about $370,000.

Suppose Company A requires $1,000,000 in capital to run the business, then the debt ratio will be 37% since the maximum debt the Company A can raise is $370,000. In this scenario, when you determine the WACC, you will apply 37% of the capital with the cost of debt, Kd, and the rest 63%, with the cost of equity, Ke.

Terminal Value

When you do the projection for your company, you need to create a cut off line for the projection. It would not be ideal for someone to try to project out the cash flow for 100 years. Not even 10 years, given that the market changes so much. The ideal time period is the period for which you feel confident to project, given that no major changes are expected in the market that will affect the future cash flow. Usually about 5 years is a good period to use.

Since you will get cash flow beyond this point, you want to determine the Present Value of the cash flow for the period after that in perpetuity. The formula is as follows:

Terminal Value = FCF(f) X (1 + g) / (WACC - g)
　FCF(f) - Free Cash Flow of the final year of projection
　g - expected perpetuity growth rate

Assuming that the industry will continue to grow, a growth rate can be used. Once you can get the terminal value, then this is discounted to be added to the Present Value of the Free Cash Flow that you projected for the first 5 years, to get to the total Present Value of the company.

16

Using the DCF Method

As seen in the above sections, there are many assumptions behind this method.

First is whether you can adequately project the future cash flow. No one knew that COVID was going to be a factor in business valuation in 2020. You, or any professional in the field, will use the best of information available at that time to make the projections. Even with the same information, different analysts or consultants can have different opinions. For example, one may think that industry will grow so the cash flow will increase, while some may think that increasing competition will squeeze the margins and will project a decrease in cash flow.

In addition, the assumptions behind the discount rate and the terminal value can also change the valuation of the company significantly.

As I started the chapter, this discounted cash flow method is most commonly used, and yet very dangerous at the same time due to the variance in assumptions that one uses. You can use this method as the base case scenario. Also, study the logic behind the assumptions to determine or refine your model. Once you do so, you can apply the other valuation methods to check whether your valuation is in line.

5

Comparable Multiples Method

I f the Discounted Cash Flow model is focusing on the intrinsic value of the company, this Comparable Multiples Method focuses on comparison with similar companies in the industry. By comparing the valuation with similar companies, you are checking to see whether your valuation from the Discounted Cash Flow is in line with the market. This method is commonly used in publicly listed companies where many comparisons are available in the market. However, this method can also be applied to private companies.

A commonly used multiple is EBITDA to Enterprise Value multiple. An EBITDA is EBIT (Earnings before Interest and Tax) + Depreciation and Amortization. It is not a true Free Cash Flow, but it reflects the company's operating cash flow by adding back the non-cash items to your EBIT.

From the above Equity Value section,
Equity Value = Enterprise Value - Debt

To determine the Enterprise Value, one can use the Discounted Cash Flow Method. However, as mentioned above, with all the assumptions that can be made, a company's valuation can vary greatly from applying different assumptions when using the DCF method. Then you need a benchmarking method to see whether your valuation using the DCF method is realistic. In publicly traded companies, this comparable multiple method can sometimes weigh more than the DCF method when determining the value of a company.

Suppose there are 7 listed companies that are in the same industry as you. Because they are all listed, you can determine their Enterprise Values from the information available in the market. For the Equity Value, you can multiply the Price per Share by the number of the outstanding shares. This will get you the total Equity Value, or the market capitalization. Then by adding the debt on their balance sheets, which are available for any publicly traded companies, to the Equity Values, you can determine the Enterprise Value of the companies in the same industry.

Then to determine the "multiple," you need to determine the EBITDA for the upcoming year. You are using the upcoming year's EBITDA, not the historical EBITDA from the past year because the market price per share is reflecting the upcoming year's projection. You can determine this yourself by making a financial projection, or just use the available analysts' projections for the listed companies.

By dividing the Enterprise Value by the projected EBITDA, you can determine the EBITDA multiple for each company in the same industry.

Suppose that the EBITDA multiple ranged from 5X to 9X for the industry, and the average was 7X. You can take the average and apply to your company. If that Company A's projected EBITDA is $100,000, then the Enterprise Value of your company can be estimated at $700,000, or 7X of the projected EBITDA. If Company A has $370,000 in debt, then you can value Company A's Equity Value at $330,000, or $700,000 - $370,000.

A more appropriate approach will be taking a closer look at the comparable companies and determining which company or companies most resemble your company. Then you can put more weight on their multiples, not the average multiple for all 7 companies in the industry. This will allow you to better reflect the market reaction to your company's value. Suppose among the 7 companies analyzed, 2 of them with 9X EBITDA multiple most resemble Company. Then, instead of applying 7X to determine the Enterprise Value, you can apply 9X, resulting in $530,000 in Equity Value, not $330,000.

However, sometimes, you do not get the ideal information from the analyses or the market. For example, the companies in your industry may have a great variance in the multiples. The multiples can range from 5X to 25X with an average of 8X. In addition, the two companies that most resemble your company may have multiples of 6X and 20X. Then which multiple do you use? In other cases, the companies may have a minus EBITDA. Many start up companies and future cash flow based companies, have negative projected EBITDA, but have a positive market capitalization. Then how do you determine the appropriate multiple to use?

Then you need to find a better, or more appropriate "multiple" for the company. For many start up industries, you can apply a revenue multiple instead of an EBITDA multiple. Since many companies in the start up industries are invested based on the future cash flow generating capability only, many companies may have negative cash flow. In this case a revenue multiple can be used, instead of an EBITDA multiple. This is commonly termed Price to Sales ratio.

Some of the other multiples commonly used are Earning per Share, or Price to Earnings ratio, and Price to Book ratio, or the Book Value multiple.

You can sometimes determine different multiples that may be most appropriate for your situation. Suppose you own a restaurant and you want to buy another restaurant. However, in the industry, there are some restaurants that make profit and some lose money. Also, the sales vary greatly depending on the size of the restaurants. Then you may want to apply Sales per Seat as a benchmarking multiple, instead of an EBITDA multiple.

In different cases, applying the most appropriate multiple, or a ratio, will get you the most appropriate value for your company. This value that you determine from the comparable multiples method can be then used to compare with the value that you get from the Discounted Cash Flow method. Ideally, the two valuations will be equal. In reality, they will not. This is when you go back and review your valuations and assumptions. Did I use the right assumptions in the DCF model? Did I select the most comparable companies when I used the multiples?

In any case, this additional method of comparing the valuations of other comparable companies can only help you refine the valuation of your company.

6

Other Commonly Used Methods

The Discounted Cash Flow method and the Comparable Multiples Method described above are the most commonly used valuation methods in the financial industry. The industry consultants also do the same. However, there are other methods that can be used. Not to replace the above two methods, but to compliment them.

Book Value

You can literally use the book value as another way to value your company. By definition, you can add all Assets on your balance sheet and subtract the liabilities, then you will get the Equity Value for your company. In this method, you are taking the balance sheet of a company and simply looking at the equity value. You can adjust certain items, such as some intangible items, but you are mainly using the balance sheet for this valuation.

This is similar to the concept of Enterprise Value being the sum of the Equity Value and the Debt. If your industry is very asset driven and has a steady cash flow, this is a method that may be appropriate. If you own a factory in an industry with very little changes and growth, this may be an appropriate valuation method.

Liquidation Value

A liquidation value is one step evolved from the above Book Value method. In this method, you are taking the book value and determining how much you will really get if you liquidate the company assets, instead of valuing it as an on-going concern. This will likely be a discount to the Book Value method, since you are only discounting the assets of a company, not the liabilities. Sometimes it may be higher. For example, if you have land that you purchased quite a while ago and you kept the value at the purchase price, and the price of land has jumped significantly since your purchase, your liquidation value may be higher than your book value. Most of the time, you will be selling your assets at a discount, and you cannot expect the liabilities owners to give you a discount.

Suppose you own a restaurant and you are trying to sell it. Your DCF model values your restaurant at $1,000,000 and your Book Value is $750,000. However, at the end of the day, no one may want to buy your restaurant. If you must sell your company because you are retiring, then you may only get $200,000 from selling your restaurant equipment and furniture, after paying off all your liabilities. This is the worst case scenario for your restaurant's valuation, but you have to keep in mind that this can be a reality if you can't find a buyer. This can be applied to your advantage if you are a buyer for this restaurant. You may be willing to pay $1,000,000 for the restaurant, but if you see that there are no other buyers, and the current owner has to sell because he is retiring, you may offer a much lower price, such as $250,000 to buy the restaurant by arguing for this Liquidation Value method.

Replacement Value

Replacement value is the value of a company if you are to start over, or replace this company, with a new one. The most critical factor will be the investment amount needed. Then you also have to apply the time value of money in building out the company. This valuation may be subjective, but sometimes it can be most appropriate.

Suppose you are a warehouse discount store company and you are expanding into a new territory. To build an advantage from the scale economy, you need to amass at least 5 stores in this territory. You already purchased 3 stores. There is a company that owns 3 stores in your territory who is willing to sell you the 3 stores. The DCF and the comparable multiple valuation methods have given you a fair value of $100 million for the 3 stores. However, the seller is asking for $150 million. In this case, you may need to determine the replacement value to see whether you should pay the $150 million price.

To replace the 3 stores, you need to purchase the land, build out the store, attain all licenses, and get all inspections passed. The total investment to be made comes out to $80 million. However, you cannot attain the scale economy by having only 3 stores that you already own. This may cost you during the construction and the inspection period of 3 years. You find out that the opportunity cost for you for not having more than 5 stores is about $50 million for the 3 year period. Then your Replacement Value for the 3 stores is $130 million, $80 million in investments and $50 million for the opportunity cost. Then you may offer up to $130 million for the 3 stores.

Recent Transactions

Sometimes, you may need to look at the recent comparable transactions to sanity check your valuation. This is similar to the comparable multiples method in that you are looking at the industry comparisons, not the intrinsic value of the company.

Suppose you are trying to sell your restaurant. You have used all the valuation methods and you find out the value of your restaurant to be between $750,000 to $1.000,000. However, you find out that recently, similar restaurants have been sold for $1,500,000 to $2,000,000. Then you may want to argue this method to value your company. There may be a lack of supply of restaurants in the market. Maybe the city is no longer issuing any new restaurant licenses. Maybe someone is developing an apartment complex that will increase the local population by 50%. Whatever the reason, if people are paying premiums to the intrinsic values in the industry, then you can apply this to your valuation and advertise the sales price of your restaurant and $1,500,000.

7

Conclusion

Now that you are aware of the commonly used valuation methods, It is important for you to determine which method or methods to use. None of the methods are wrong, at the same time, none of them are perfect. You can even take the average of the valuations you get.

I have described the methods with some examples that are appropriate. However, at the end of the day, it is always your money. If you are selling, you want the highest valuation possible. If you are buying, you want the lowest valuation possible. If you can convince the other party of your valuation using the above methods, you can be a winner. If you are a stock market investor, you want to determine the target price of the company that you are interested in. Or you want to just understand the logic behind the recommendations that the analysts are providing. Whether you are a stock market investor or a private business owner, I hope that you are one step closer to your goals after reading this book.

This book should have given you some understanding of the valuation methods that are commonly used by the professionals in the industry. Always keep in mind that the methods will develop over time. Keep an eye out for any latest updates and developments. However, always be firm on your belief in the valuation methods and the fundamentals behind them.